Confirmat [W9-BHE-618]
of Joram Rouerr Coxworth
from Hana

10 13 96

Donald K. McKim
April 6, 2006

BREAKFAST WITH THE SAINTS

Breakfast with the Saints

Daily Readings from Great Christians

SELECTED BY LAVONNE NEFF

CHARIS

Servant Publications
Ann Arbor, Michigan

© 1996 by Servant Publications
All rights reserved.

Charis Books is an imprint of Servant Publications especially designed to serve Roman Catholics.

Scripture texts used in this work are taken from *The Holy Bible: New Revised Standard Version,* © 1989 by the Division of Christian Education of the National Council of the Churches of Christ in the USA. All rights reserved.

Excerpts from pages 327, 312-13, 198 from *Devotional Classics* by Richard J. Foster and James Bryan Smith. © 1990, 1991, 1993 by RENOVARE, Inc. Reprinted by permission of HarperCollins Publishers, Inc.

Other acknowledgments are in the first appendix.

Published by Servant Publications
P.O. Box 8617
Ann Arbor, Michigan 48107

Cover design: Left Coast Design, Portland, OR
Interior illustrations: Steve Erspamer. Used by permission, Liturgy Training Publications

96 97 98 99 00 10 9 8 7 6 5 4 3 2 1

Printed in the United States of America
ISBN 0-89283-970-8

All the flowers God has made are beautiful. The rose in its glory and the lily in its whiteness do not rob the tiny violet of its sweet smell, or the daisy of its charming simplicity. I saw that if all these lesser blooms wanted to be roses instead, nature would lose the gaiety of her springtide dress—there would be no little flowers to make a pattern over the countryside. And so it is with the world of souls, which is the Lord's garden. He wanted to have great saints to be his lilies and roses, but he has made lesser saints as well; and these lesser ones must be content to rank as daisies and violets, lying at his feet and giving pleasure to his eye like that. Perfection consists simply in doing his will, and being just what he wants us to be.

ST. THÉRÈSE OF LISIEUX

I believe in the communion of saints...

These words from the Apostles' Creed proclaim a mind-boggling truth: Everywhere in the world, and at all times throughout history, I have brothers and sisters, mothers and fathers, aunts and uncles, daughters and sons; friends, teachers, counselors, and helpers; people with whom to laugh and also to weep, people who care about me and who stand ready to help.

Who are these people? Many of them have been honored by the church, and we call them Saint or Blessed or Holy. Many more are known only to God; we can also call them saints, if we like. That is how St. Paul addressed all Christian believers.

Here is a collection of 120 morning readings by—or sometimes about—saints that the church has named. Some are famous; many are nearly forgotten. Included here are men and women, hermits and parents, theologians and peasants, young adults and centenarians, saints who were contemporaries of Jesus and saints who lived during the Industrial Revolution.

Since saints are all unique, alike only in their deep love for God, these selections come in many topics and styles—prayers, poems, stories, admonitions, words of encouragement, reflections, personal experiences....

With each reading is a note about the saint who provided it. So settle back at the start of your day, pour yourself a cup of coffee, and make a new friend as you enjoy your *Breakfast with the Saints*.

St. Aelred of Rievaulx (1110-1167), a Cistercian abbot in northern England, wrote several treatises and biographies. He was known for his gentleness and friendliness.

Love Is Not a Feeling

Our love of God must not be measured by the passing feelings we experience that are not controlled by the will. Rather, we must judge our feelings by the enduring quality of the will itself. For loving God means that we join our will to God's will. It means that our will consents to whatever God's will commands. It means that we have only one reason for wishing anything—that we know God wills it. Feelings and emotions are for God to bestow when and where and to whom he wills. It is not for us to seek them or even to ask for them. If God should suddenly remove them from us, our wills must accept his will. For the one who loves God is the one who bears patiently with all that God does, and is zealous in carrying out God's commands.

St. Aidan was Bishop of Lindisfarne and a missionary to northern England during the seventh century. Some eighty years after his death, St. Bede the Venerable told this story about him.

The Worth of a Human Being

∞

The king gave Bishop Aidan a splendid horse, which Aidan could ride—though he was used to walking—when crossing rivers or when some other necessity required it. Soon afterward a poor man met the bishop and asked for money. Aidan dismounted and ordered that the horse, still bearing the king's caparison, be given to the poor man. For Aidan was very compassionate, a great friend to the poor.

The king learned what had happened. As he and the bishop were going in together to dinner, the king said, "What were you thinking of, my lord bishop, in giving a poor man that royal horse? It was meant for you. Do we not have many lesser horses that would make adequate gifts for the poor? Why, then, did you give away the horse we had especially chosen for you?"

The bishop immediately replied, "What are you saying, O King? Is that son of a mare dearer to you than the Son of God?"

Blessed Alcuin (ca. 735-804), an English theologian and educator, became Charlemagne's ecclesiastical adviser and head of his palace school.

We Seek Your Face

∞

Eternal Light, shine into our hearts;
Eternal Goodness, deliver us from evil;
Eternal Power, be our support;
Eternal Wisdom, scatter the darkness of our
    ignorance;
Eternal Pity, have mercy upon us—
    so that with all our heart and mind and soul and
    strength
    we may seek your face
    and be brought by your infinite mercy into your
    holy presence,
    through Jesus Christ our Lord.

St. Alphonsus Liguori (1696-1787) was a sensible, sweet-tempered man who spent his life immersed in political and spiritual trials. Founder of the Redemptorists, he was a lawyer, a bishop, and a brilliant moral theologian.

How to Resist Temptation

*W*hen an evil thought comes into the mind, we must immediately try to turn our thoughts to God or at least to something that is not sinful. But the first rule is this: We must instantly call upon the names of Jesus and Mary, and continue to call upon them until the temptation ceases. If we trust in ourselves, we are lost. If we trust in God, we can do all things.

St. Ambrose (ca. 340-397) was a government official in the Roman Empire when he was called by popular acclamation to be Bishop of Milan. He was a friend of St. Augustine.

The Happy Life
∞

The wise are not broken by bodily ills,
    nor are they disturbed by misfortunes;
      but they remain happy even amid troubles.
Bodily adversities do not diminish the gift of the happy life
    or take away anything from its sweetness.
For life's happiness does not lie in bodily pleasure,
    but in a conscience pure of every stain of sin,
      and in a mind aware that the good is also the pleasurable,
      even though it is harsh,
      and that the shameful does not give delight,
      even though it is sweet.

St. Anselm of Canterbury (ca. 1033-1109) spent many years in exile from his archdiocese for antagonizing the political powers. He has been called the father of scholasticism. This is from a famous address—*Proslogion*—in which St. Anselm discusses faith and understanding.

I Believe So That I May Understand
∞

*T*each me to seek you,
 and when I seek you, show yourself to me;
 for I cannot seek you unless you teach me,
 or find you unless you show yourself to me.
Let me seek you by desiring you,
 and desire you by seeking you.
Let me find you by loving you,
 and love you when I find you.
I do not seek to understand so that I can believe,
 but I believe so that I may understand.
For this too I believe:
Unless I believe, I shall not understand.

St. Anthony the Great (251-356), an Egyptian monk who founded communities of hermits in the desert, has been called the father of Christian monasticism. At the age of 104 he traveled to Alexandria to preach against heretics. Many stories were collected about him.

Lord, Why
∞

When Abba Anthony thought about the depth of God's judgments, he asked,

Lord, how is it that some die when they are young,
while others drag on to extreme old age?
Why are there those who are poor
and those who are rich?
Why do the wicked prosper,
and why are the just in need?
He heard a voice answering him,

Anthony, keep your attention on yourself;
these things are according to God's judgment,
and you do not need to know anything about them.

St. Antony of Padua (1195-1231), known today as the saint who helps people find lost objects, was a famous preacher and teacher. A Franciscan, he appears in *The Little Flowers of St. Francis.*

The Fish Came First

O nce the blessed Antony was in Rimini, where there were many heretics. Wishing to bring them back to the light of the true faith and to the way of truth, he preached to them for many days about the Holy Scriptures. But they refused to give him a hearing.

So St. Antony, under the Lord's inspiration, one day went to the mouth of a river and began in the Lord's name to summon the fish as if to a sermon. And behold! There immediately gathered before St. Antony a multitude of fish, great and small, all holding their heads just a little bit above water. And so to them he began to preach. The longer St. Antony preached, the more the throng of fish increased.

At this miracle the people of the city flocked together. Filled with remorse, all sat down at St. Antony's feet so that he might preach to them. St. Antony preached so wonderfully about the Catholic faith that he converted all the heretics present, and the faithful he sent away with his blessing, rejoicing and strengthened. The fish too he dismissed all joyous and exultant; amid wonderful nods of satisfaction they departed to their various parts of the ocean.

16

St. Athanasius (ca. 297-373), because he dedicated his life to fighting heresy, was known by the saying, "Athanasius against the world." Though Bishop of Alexandria, he spent many years in exile. This is from his famous work, *On the Incarnation*.

The End of Darkness
∞

Since the Savior has come among us, idolatry not only has no longer increased, but what there was is diminishing and gradually coming to an end.

Not only does the wisdom of the Greeks no longer advance, but what there is is now fading away.

Demons, so far from cheating any more by illusions and prophecies and magic arts—if they so much as dare to make the attempt—are put to shame by the sign of the cross.

For as when the sun is come, darkness no longer prevails, so now that the Word of God is come, the darkness of idols prevails no more, and all parts of the world in every direction are illumined by his teaching.

St. Augustine of Canterbury was sent by Pope Gregory the Great to England to convert the Anglo-Saxon pagans. He became the first Archbishop of Canterbury and died in England in 605. St. Bede the Venerable tells of his mission.

Walking the Walk
∞

Augustine and his companions began to reproduce the apostolic way of life of the early church. They practiced unceasing prayer, vigil, and fasting. They preached the Word of Life to whomever they could. They paid no attention to worldly things, receiving from those whom they taught only such provisions as seemed necessary. They themselves practiced everything they preached, and they were willing to endure any hardships and even to die for the truth they proclaimed.

Very soon many people came to believe and were baptized, admiring the simplicity of their innocent lives and the sweetness of their heavenly teaching. The king also was captivated by the holy men's pure lives and gracious promises, confirmed by many miracles. He believed and was baptized. And then many others began to flock every day to hear the Word. They forsook pagan rites and joined themselves through belief to the unity of the holy church of Christ.

St. Augustine of Hippo (354-430) was the greatest of the Latin fathers. After a midlife conversion, he became Bishop of Hippo in North Africa. He founded religious communities, preached, and wrote many books, including *The Confessions*, from which this prayer is taken.

Late Have I Loved You

Late have I loved you, beauty so old and so new: late have I loved you. And see, you were within and I was in the external world and sought you there, and in my unlovely state I plunged into those lovely created things which you made. You were with me, and I was not with you. The lovely things kept me far from you, though if they did not have their existence in you, they had no existence at all. You called and cried out loud and shattered my deafness. You were radiant and resplendent, you put to flight my blindness. You were fragrant, and I drew in my breath and now pant after you. I tasted you, and I feel but hunger and thirst for you. You touched me, and I am set on fire to attain the peace which is yours.

St. Barsanuphius was a sixth-century anchorite (hermit) at Gaza.

How to Tell a Food Addict
∞

*I*f you wish to find out whether you are addicted to the passion of gluttony, you can find it out in the following manner. If food captures your thought, so that you cannot resist it, you are a glutton. If you are not possessed by it and partake freely of all kinds of food to the extent your body requires it, you are not a glutton. Almighty God has given sweetness to every kind of food, and a person who receives it with thankfulness suffers no harm. But passionate attachment should always be avoided, for it does harm to the soul.

St. Basil the Great (329-379), Bishop of Caesarea, was a great preacher and theologian. Known as the father of Eastern monasticism, he is one of the Three Holy Hierarchs of the Eastern Church. He wrote this in a letter to a monk who had sinned.

God Will Forgive
∞

*B*e aware of God's compassion, that it heals with oil and wine. Do not lose hope of salvation. Remember what is written—

the one who falls shall rise again,
and the one who turns away shall turn again;
the wounded is healed;
the one caught by wild beasts escapes;
the one who confesses is not rejected.

For the Lord does not want the sinner to die, but to return and live. There is still time for endurance, time for patience, time for healing, time for change. Have you slipped? Rise up. Have you sinned? Cease. Do not stand among sinners, but leap aside. For when you turn back and weep, then you will be saved.

21

St. Benedict (ca. 480–ca. 547), a layperson, became a hermit to escape dissolute Rome. Disciples soon joined him, and eventually he founded the monastery of Monte Cassino. His Rule, from which this is taken, became the norm for Western monasticism.

Brief and Humble Prayers
∞

When we make application to men in high positions we do not presume to do so without reverence and humility. How much more, then, are we bound to entreat God, the Lord of all, with all humility and devout purity of heart? We must recognize that we are heard not for our much speaking, but for our purity of heart and tears of contrition. Therefore our prayer must be brief and pure—unless it chance to be prolonged with the inspiration of God's grace.

St. Bernard of Clairvaux (1090-1153) is known as a mystic and an activist. He established sixty-eight Cistercian monasteries, preached a crusade, and assisted at church councils. This is from *On the Love of God*.

The Four Stages of Love
∞

What are the four stages of love?

First, we love ourselves for our own sake. Since we are unspiritual and worldly, we cannot be interested in anything that does not relate to ourselves.

Second, when we begin to see that we cannot get along by ourselves, we begin to seek God for our own sakes. We love God, but only for our own interests.

Third, if we begin to worship God and come into his presence repeatedly by meditating, reading, praying, and obeying, little by little we come to know God through experience. By tasting how sweet the Lord is, we begin to love God, not for our own sake, but for himself.

I am not certain that the fourth stage of love, in which we love ourselves only for the sake of God, may be perfectly attained in this life. But whenever it happens, we experience the joy of the Lord and forget ourselves in a wonderful way. We are, for those moments, of one mind and one spirit with God.

St. Bonaventure (1221-1274) was a cardinal and a bishop who was also a great mystical and scholastic theologian. This is from the beginning of *The Journey of the Mind to God.*

Help for Happiness
∽

Since happiness is nothing but the enjoyment of the Supreme Good, and since the Supreme Good is above us, we cannot be happy unless we rise beyond ourselves. Since we cannot reach above ourselves in our own strength, we must be helped by supernatural strength, lifted up by a higher power that stoops to raise us. However much we structure our inner lives and make progress, it does us no good unless our efforts are accompanied by help from on high.

Divine aid is available for those who seek it with a devout and humble heart; this is done by fervent prayer. Prayer is, therefore, the source and origin of every upward journey toward God. Let us each, then, turn to prayer and say to our Lord God: "Lead me, O Lord, on your path, that I may walk in your truth."

St. Braulio of Saragossa was a seventh-century Spanish bishop known for his devotion to the poor.

Don't Give Up!
∞

Our endurance must go beyond confessing the name of Christian when punishment by sword and fire is threatened. We must also endure such temptations as differences in customs, insults from those who disobey God, and the barbs of wicked tongues. In fact, no occupation is without its dangers. But who will guide the ship through the waves if the pilot quits his post? Who will guard against wolves if the shepherd does not watch? Or who will drive away the robber if sleep removes the watchman from the lookout point?

Stick by the work entrusted to you and the task you have undertaken.

Observe justice and show mercy.

Hate the sins, not the sinners.

Strengthen the weak and correct the proud.

Even if tribulation brings us more than we can endure, let us not be afraid as if we were resisting in our own strength. We must pray that God will give us "the way out" (1 Cor 10:13).

St. Brigid (ca. 450-ca. 525), a patron saint of Ireland, is said to have been baptized by St. Patrick. She founded the monastery of Kildare, which later included both men and women. Cogitosus wrote a *Life of Brigid* in the seventh century.

All Life Serves God

Once a solitary wild boar which was being hunted ran out from the woods, and in its headlong flight was brought suddenly into the herd of pigs that belonged to the most blessed Brigid. She noticed its arrival among her pigs, and she blessed it. Thereupon it lost its fear and settled down among the herd. See how brute beasts and animals could oppose neither her bidding nor her wish, but served her tamely and humbly.

On another day the blessed Brigid felt a tenderness for some ducks that she saw swimming on the water and occasionally taking wing. She commanded them to come to her. A great flock of them flew on feathered wings toward her, without any fear, as if they were humans under obedience. When she had touched them with her hand and caressed them, she released them and let them fly into the sky. She praised the Creator of all things greatly, to whom all life is subject, and for the service of whom all life is given.

BRI
GID

St. Caedmon, who lived during the seventh century, has been called the father of English sacred poetry. A herdsman of the monastery at Whitby, he was made a monk in honor of his poetic gifts. This is his only surviving hymn, also known as "Caedmon's Hymn."

Praise to the Creator

$\mathcal{N}$ow must we praise the Guardian of heaven,
The power and conception of the Lord,
And all his works, as he, eternal Lord,
Father of glory, started every wonder.
First he created heaven as a roof,
The holy Maker, for the sons of men.
Then the eternal Keeper of mankind
Furnished the earth below, the land for men,
Almighty God and everlasting Lord.

St. Caesarius of Arles (470-543) became an archbishop at age thirty. A popular preacher, he founded a monastery for women.

Read the Scriptures at Home

∞

If you want the sacred writings to become sweet to you and the divine commands to help you as they should, withdraw from worldly occupations for several hours to reread the divine words in your homes and to dedicate yourselves entirely to God's mercy. Merchants do not limit themselves to just one source of income; they look for many ways to increase their profits. Farmers sow more than one kind of seed in order to be able to provide enough food for themselves and their family. Likewise, your spiritual profit should not be limited to hearing the divine lessons in church. At home also you should engage in sacred reading, even for several hours an evening when the days are short. Thus you will store spiritual wheat in the storehouse of your heart, and Scriptural pearls in the treasury of your souls.

St. Catherine of Bologna was a fifteenth-century nun who began community life as a baker and ended as a visionary. She devoted her life to interceding for sinners, and she was known for her powers of healing.

Avoid Extremes

Sometimes the devil inspires souls with an inordinate zeal for a certain virtue or some special pious exercise, so that they will be motivated by their passion to practice it more and more.

Sometimes, on the other hand, the devil permits souls to become discouraged, wearied, and disgusted so that they neglect everything.

It is as necessary to overcome the one snare as the other.

St. Catherine of Genoa (1447-1510) had been unhappily married for ten years when she persuaded her husband to join her in a ministry to the sick. From that day forth, she combined hard work with intense mystical spirituality. This is from her *Life and Teachings*.

Growth and Imperfection

∞

At times I have thought that my love was complete, but later, as my sight grew clearer, I became aware that I had many imperfections. I did not recognize them at first because God's love for me has it planned that I will achieve complete love little by little, for the sake of keeping me humble so as to be tolerable to myself and others!

Every day I feel the motes in my eyes being removed as God's pure love casts them out. We cannot see these imperfections because if we saw them, we could not bear the sight. Thus, God lets us imagine that we are complete. But never does God cease to remove them. From time to time I feel that I am growing only to see that I still have a long way to go. The imperfections become visible to me in the mirror of God's Truth, of his Pure Love where everything I thought was straight appears crooked.

St. Catherine of Siena (1347-1380) is one of only two women declared a Doctor of the Church. A third-order Dominican, she was both a mystic and a politician to whom popes listened.

Deep Sea, Consuming Fire

~

You, O eternal Trinity, are a deep sea, into which the more I enter the more I find, and the more I find the more I seek. The soul cannot be satiated in your abyss, for she continually hungers after you, the eternal Trinity, desiring to see you with the light of your light. As the hart desires the springs of living water, so my soul desires to leave the prison of this dark body and see you in truth.

O abyss, O eternal Godhead, O sea profound, what more could you give me than yourself! You are the fire that ever burns without being consumed; you consume in your heat all the soul's self-love; you are the fire which takes away cold; with your light you illuminate me so that I may know all your truth. Clothe me, clothe me with yourself, Eternal Truth, so that I may run this mortal life with true obedience, and with the light of your most holy faith.

St. Clare of Assisi (1193-1253) was an early follower of St. Francis. She founded the first convent of Franciscan nuns, the Poor Clares, at San Damiano near Assisi. Many came to her there for healing and intercessory prayer. The following was excerpted from a letter from St. Clare to her sister, Agnes, who was also an abbess.

A Letter to Agnes
∞

O ur flesh is not made of bronze, and our strength is not that of stone. On the contrary, we are fragile and inclined to all kinds of bodily weakness. So, my dear friend, I ask you in the Lord's name to be wise and prudent. Turn away from the rigid abstinence—which is not only foolish but also impossible—that I hear you have undertaken. Turn away so that in this life you can witness to the Lord, and so that you can give the Lord your reasonable worship—a living sacrifice seasoned with salt.

CLARE

St. Clement of Rome was Bishop of Rome during the last decade of the first century. He died in 101.

A Prayer for the World

∾

We beg you, Lord, to help and protect us.
Deliver the oppressed,
   pity the unnoticed,
   raise the fallen,
   show yourself to the needy,
   heal the sick,
   bring back those of your people who have gone astray,
   feed the hungry,
   lift up the weak,
   remove the prisoners' chains.
May every nation come to know
   that you alone are God,
   that Jesus Christ is your Child,
   that we are your people, the sheep that you pasture.

St. Columba (ca. 521-597) is the most famous Scottish saint. He founded churches and monasteries in Ireland before founding Iona, from which he preached the gospel throughout Scotland.

A Traveler's Prayer

*T*he path I walk, Christ walks it.
May the land in which I am be without sorrow.
May the Trinity protect me wherever I stay,
    Father, Son, and Holy Spirit.
May bright angels walk with me—dear presence—in every
    dealing.
May I arrive at every place; may I return home.
May the way in which I spend be a way without loss.
May every path before me be smooth.
May man, woman, and child welcome me.
A truly good journey! Well does the fair Lord show us a path.

St. Columban (ca. 543-615) was an Irish founder of monasteries throughout Europe, including Luxeuil (present-day France) and Bobbio (present-day Italy). This prayer has been attributed to him.

Root Out Evil, Sow Good

∞

O Lord God, destroy and root out whatever the Adversary plants in me, so that with my sins destroyed you may sow understanding and good work in my mouth and heart; so that in act and in truth I may serve only you and know how to fulfill the commandments of Christ and to seek yourself.

Give me memory, give me love, give me chastity, give me faith, give me all things which you know belong to the profit of my soul.

O Lord, work good in me, and provide me with what you know that I need. Amen.

St. Crispina was an upper-class African married woman and the mother of several children when she was beheaded for her faith in 304.

The Martyrdom of Crispina
∞

*T*he proconsul Anullinus said: "If you refuse to worship our venerable gods, I shall order your head cut off."

"I should be very happy to lose my head for the sake of my God," replied Crispina, "for I refuse to sacrifice to these silly deaf and dumb statues. My God, who is now and will be for ever, ordered my birth. He gave me salvation through the saving waters of baptism. He is at my side, helping me and strengthening me in everything so that I will not commit sacrilege."

Anullinus read the sentence from a tablet: "Seeing that Crispina has persisted in scandalous superstition and refuses to sacrifice to our gods, I order her executed with the sword."

Crispina replied: "I bless God who has so chosen to free me from your hands. Thanks be to God!" And making the sign of the cross on her forehead and stretching out her neck, she was beheaded for the name of the Lord Jesus Christ.

St. Cyprian of Carthage (ca. 200-258) was a North African bishop during a time of persecution and division within the church; he was beheaded under the Emperor Valerian. He dedicated his life to Christian unity. This is taken from *The Unity of the Catholic Church.*

Christian Unity

∞

The church is a single whole, though she spreads far and wide into a multitude of churches. We may compare her to the sun, with many rays but one light; or to a tree, with many branches but one firmly rooted trunk. When many streams flow from one spring, unity is preserved in the source. Pluck a ray from the body of the sun, and its unity allows no division of the light. Break a branch from the tree, and when it is broken off it will not bud. Cut a stream off from its spring, and when it is cut off it dries up. In the same way the church, bathed in the light of the Lord, spreads her rays throughout the world; yet the light everywhere diffused is one light, and the unity of the body is not broken. In the abundance of her plenty she stretches her branches over the whole earth; far and wide she pours her generously flowing streams. Yet there is one head, one source, one mother boundlessly fruitful.

St. Cyril of Jerusalem (ca. 315-386) was a theologian, a writer, and Bishop of Jerusalem. Sixteen of his thirty-five years as bishop he spent in exile. These are some of his reflections in *On the Mysteries*.

The Body and Blood of Christ

∞

Jesus once changed water into wine by a word of command at Cana of Galilee. Should we not believe that he changes wine into blood? Let us have full assurance that we partake of Christ's body and blood. For in the symbol of bread it is his body that is given to you, and in the symbol of wine it is his blood, so that by receiving the body and blood of Christ you may become one body and one blood with him. Thus we become Christ-bearers, since his body and his blood are spread throughout our limbs.

So do not think of them as mere bread and wine; as our Lord said, they are body and blood. And if the senses suggest otherwise, let faith confirm you. Do not judge on the basis of taste, but on the basis of faith be assured beyond all doubt that you have been allowed to receive the body and blood of Christ.

St. Diadochos of Photike (ca. 400-ca. 486), a bishop in northern Greece, was a mystic who emphasized the heart as well as the intellect. He wrote *On Spiritual Knowledge and Discrimination*.

Fully Warmed by Grace

∽

When we stand out of doors in winter at dawn, facing the east, the front of our body is warmed by the sun, while the back is still cold because the sun is not on it. Similarly, the heart of those who are beginning to experience the Spirit's energy is only partially warmed by God's grace. While the mind begins to produce spiritual thoughts, the outer parts of the heart continue to produce worldly thoughts, since the members of the heart have not yet all become fully aware of the light of God's grace shining upon them. But when we begin to carry out God's commands with our whole heart, we become fully conscious of the light of grace. The flames of grace consume our thoughts; grace sweetens our heart in the peace of uninterrupted love; grace enables us to think spiritual, not worldly, thoughts. These effects of grace are always present in those who are approaching perfection and who constantly remember the Lord Jesus in their heart.

St. Dimitrii of Rostov (1641-1709) was a Russian bishop celebrated as a preacher and writer.

Come, My Light

∞

Come, my Light, and illumine my darkness.
Come, my Life, and revive me from death.
Come, my Physician, and heal my wounds.
Come, Flame of divine love, and burn up the thorns of my sins,
    kindling my heart with the flame of thy love.
Come, my King, sit upon the throne of my heart and
    reign there.
For thou alone art my King and my Lord.

St. Dionysius the Areopagite is the name adopted by a late-fifth-or early-sixth-century Greek mystical theologian, after a Christian convert mentioned in Acts 17:34. He is sometimes known as Pseudo-Dionysius.

The Radiance of the Divine Darkness

∞

*L*eave the senses and the workings of the mind,
    and all that the senses and the mind can perceive,
    and all that is not and all that is;
    and through *unknowing* reach out (so far as this is possible)
    toward oneness with the One
    who is beyond all being and all knowledge.
In this way, through an uncompromising, absolute, and pure
    detachment from yourself and from all things,
    transcending all things and released from all things,
    you will be led upward
    toward that radiance of the divine darkness
    that is beyond all being.

St. Dismas is the name traditionally given to the good thief, one of the two criminals crucified with Jesus. Nothing is known about him, except that he had enormous faith to trust in someone who was about to die. His story is told in Luke 23:32-33, 39-43.

Remember Me

Two others also, who were criminals, were led away to be put to death with [Jesus]. When they came to the place that is called The Skull, they crucified Jesus there with the criminals, one on his right and one on his left.

One of the criminals who were hanged there kept deriding him and saying, "Are you not the Messiah? Save yourself and us!" But the other rebuked him, saying, "Do you not fear God, since you are under the same sentence of condemnation? And we indeed have been condemned justly, for we are getting what we deserve for our deeds, but this man has done nothing wrong." Then he said, "Jesus, remember me when you come into your kingdom."

Jesus replied, "Truly I tell you, today you will be with me in Paradise."

St. Dominic (ca. 1170-1221), Spanish founder of the Order of Preachers (Dominicans), spent much of his life fighting heresy and yet still was known for his kindly sympathy. This description is from *The Nine Ways of Prayer of St. Dominic* written by one of his followers.

Praying the Scriptures

∞

When Dominic was traveling, he would steal sudden moments of prayer, unobtrusively, and would stand with his whole mind instantaneously concentrated on heaven, and soon you would have heard him pronouncing, with the utmost enjoyment and relish, some lovely text from the very heart of sacred Scripture, which he would seem to have drawn fresh from the Savior's wells. The brethren used to be greatly moved by this example, when they saw their father and master praying in this way, and the more devout among them found it the best possible instruction in how to pray continuously and reverently.

DOMINIC

St. Edmund of Abingdon (1180-1240) was Archbishop of Canterbury and a theology professor at Oxford. One of his first official acts was to threaten King Henry III with excommunication. Not surprisingly, Henry opposed his canonization in 1247.

God's Will is Holiness

$\mathcal{A}$ perfect life is a life of honor, humility, and love,
and an honorable life is to will to do God's will.
Before doing anything, ask yourself if it is God's will:
whether it is thinking in your heart,
speaking with your mouth, seeing with your eyes,
hearing with your ears, smelling with your nose,
tasting with your tongue, touching with your hands,
walking or standing, lying or sitting.
If it is God's will, then do it with all your might.
If it is not God's will, then die rather than do it.
If you ask me, "What is God's will?" I will answer:
"God's will is that you become holy."

St. Elizabeth Bayley Seton (1774-1821) was the first American-born saint. Widowed with five children, she founded the Daughters of Charity of St. Joseph to care for orphans, the sick, and parochial schools.

The Joy of Reconciliation

∽

When our corrupted nature overpowers, when we are sick of ourselves, weakened on all sides,
  discouraged by repeated lapses, wearied with sin and sorrow,
  we gently, sweetly lay the whole account at his feet.
Reconciled and encouraged by his appointed representative,
  yet trembling and conscious of our imperfect dispositions,
  we draw near the sacred fountain.
Scarcely the expanded heart receives its longing desire,
  than wrapped in his love, covered with his righteousness,
  we are no longer the same.

St. Ephraem of Syria (ca. 306-373), a layperson, was the greatest theologian, preacher, and poet of the Syrian church.

Glory to You, Lord
∞

*W*hat shall I give you, Lord, in return for all your kindness?
Glory to you for your love.
Glory to you for your mercy.
Glory to you for your patience.
Glory to you for forgiving us all our sins.
Glory to you for coming to save our souls.
Glory to you for your incarnation in the virgin's womb.
Glory to you for your bonds.
Glory to you for receiving the cut of the lash.
Glory to you for accepting mockery.
Glory to you for your crucifixion.
Glory to you for your burial.
Glory to you for your resurrection.
Glory to you who were preached to men and women.
Glory to you in whom they believed.
Glory to you who were taken up into heaven.
Glory to you who sit in great glory at the Father's right hand.
Glory to you whose will it is that the sinner should be saved
    through your great mercy and compassion.

St. Francis Xavier (1506-1552) was one of the first followers of St. Ignatius Loyola. He became a missionary to many countries in Asia.

Remember All Nations

∞

O God of all nations of the earth, remember the multitudes who, though created in your image, do not know you, and do not know the dying of your Son, their Savior, Jesus Christ.

Grant that by the prayers and work of your holy church they may be delivered from all ignorance and unbelief and brought to worship you; through him whom you have sent to be the resurrection and the life of all people, your Son Jesus Christ, our Lord.

St. Francis of Assisi (1181-1226), one of the church's most beloved saints, is remembered as the nature-loving founder of the Friars Minor (Franciscans). St. Francis received the marks of Christ's crucifixion in his hands and side, and was a deacon but not a priest.

Praise for All Created Things
∞

$\mathcal{P}$raise to my Lord God for all created things,
   especially our brother the sun,
     who brings us the day and who brings us the light:
     fair is he and shines with a great splendor.
O Lord, he points us to you.
Praise to my Lord for our sister the moon,
     and for the stars, which he has set clear and lovely in the sky.
Praise to my Lord for our sister water,
     who is very useful to us and humble and precious and clean.
Praise to my Lord for our brother fire,
     through whom you give us light in the darkness;
     he is bright and pleasant and very mighty and strong.
Praise to my Lord for our mother the earth,
     who sustains us and keeps us,
     and brings forth abundant fruits
     and flowers of many colors and grass.

St. Francis de Sales (1567-1622), bishop of Geneva and preacher to the disaffected, won converts through the force of his love. He is the patron saint of journalists and other writers. This is from his *Introduction to the Devout Life.*

Devotion Beautifies Work
∞

Devotion must be practiced in different ways by the gentleman, the worker, the servant, the prince, the widow, the young girl, and the married woman. The practice of devotion must also be adapted to the strength, activities, and duties of each particular person. True devotion does us no harm whatsoever, but instead perfects all things. When it goes contrary to one's lawful vocation, it is undoubtedly false. "The bee," Aristotle says, "extracts honey out of flowers without hurting them" and leaves them as whole and fresh as it finds them. True devotion does better still. It not only does no injury to one's vocation or occupation, but on the contrary adorns and beautifies it. All kinds of precious stones take on greater luster when dipped into honey, each according to its color. So also every vocation becomes more agreeable when united with devotion. Care of one's family is rendered more peaceable, love of husband and wife more sincere, service of one's prince more faithful, and every type of employment more pleasant and agreeable.

St. Fulgentius of Ruspe (467-533), an African bishop, was a monk, a disciple of his fellow African bishop, St. Augustine of Hippo, and a writer. He was banished for fifteen years to Sardinia.

A Prayer for Truth

We beg you, O God, the God of Truth,
　that whatever we do not know of things we ought to know,
　you will teach us;
　that whatever we know of truth,
　you will confirm us within;
　that wherever we are mistaken, as all must be,
　you will correct us;
　that at whatever truths we stumble,
　you will establish us;
　and that from all things false and all hurtful knowledge,
　you will evermore deliver us,
　through Jesus Christ our Lord.

St. Gertrude the Great (ca. 1256-ca. 1302) was a religious at the monastery of Helfta in Saxony. At the age of 25 she had a powerful conversion experience about which she wrote until her death.

My Heart's Beloved

∽

Ah! Jesus, my heart's beloved, surely no spiritual plant can bear fruit unless it is drenched in the dew of your Spirit, unless it is nourished by the strength of your love. May it please you then to take pity on me, to receive me in the arms of your love, and to warm me through and through by your Spirit. Here are my body and my soul: I give them to you.

My beloved, my beloved, pour out on me your blessing. Open me up to the fullness of your sweetness. It is with heart and soul that I long for you and that I beg you to possess me, you alone. Ah! I am yours, and you are mine! Make me grow, with ever-renewing spiritual fervor, in your living love. By your grace make me flower like the lilies of the valley on the banks of flowing streams.

St. Godric was an English seafarer who then became a hermit for sixty years until his death in 1170. He was known for his second sight and his power over animals.

A Morning Prayer
∞

Holy Mary, Virgin clean,
Mother of Jesus, the Nazarene,
Me, your Godric, help today.
Shield me, hear me, when I pray,
That with you eternally
In God's Kingdom I may be.

St. Gregory VII (ca. 1020-1085), whose given name was Hildebrand, was a strong pope famous for reforming the church, enforcing celibacy in the West, resisting kings, and eliminating corrupt financial practices.

The Burden of Leadership
∽

As to my situation, about which you inquire so eagerly, it is this: Against my will I took command of the ship when she was tossed upon a troubled sea by violent storms, buffeted by the whirlwind and by waves as high as heaven. Yet she courageously steers her dangerous course around rocks hidden or towering into the air. The Holy Roman Church is daily and constantly buffeted by myriad temptations, persecutions, and heresies, and she must steer around the secret or open hostility of princes and emperors. To meet all these and many other dangers and provide against them is under God my special care and duty; by these cares I am consumed day and night, by them I am torn in pieces. Thus I live, and by God's help I will continue so to live.

St. Gregory Palamas (ca. 1296-1359) was Archbishop of Thessalonica and a mystical theologian known for his teaching on interior prayer and divine revelation.

Endless Light
∞

*I*n mystical contemplation a person sees neither with the mind nor with the body, but with the Spirit. He knows with complete certainty that he sees supernaturally a light that outshines all other light, but he does not know through what organ he sees this light; for the ways of the Spirit, through which he sees, are unsearchable.

This is what St. Paul affirmed, when "whether in the body or out of the body I do not know" he "heard things that are not to be told, that no mortal is permitted to repeat" (2 Cor 12:3-4). Paul's happy and joyful experience took the form of light—a light of revelation, but not one that revealed objects of sense perception. It was a light without boundaries below or above or to the sides. He saw no limit whatever to the light that shone around him: it was like a sun infinitely brighter and greater than the universe. And in the midst of this light he himself stood, having become nothing but eye.

St. Gregory of Nazianzen (ca. 329-390), one of the Three Holy Hierarchs of the Eastern church, was the son of two saints, St. Gregory the Elder (a bishop) and St. Nonna. He became Bishop of Constantinople for a few months, but he retired quickly and returned to writing.

Make Me Able

∞

I rise and pledge myself to God
to do no deed at all of dark.
This day shall be his sacrifice
and I, unmoved, my passions' lord.
I blush to be so old and foul
and yet to stand before his table.
You know what I would do, O Christ;
O then, to do it make me able.

St. Gregory of Nyssa (ca. 335-ca. 395) was the little brother of St. Basil the Great and St. Macrina, whose biography he wrote. Their parents and grandparents were also saints. Gregory was a bishop, a theologian, and a writer. This is from *The Life of Moses.*

This Brilliant Darkness

The vision of God does not come through sight or hearing or any of the ordinary senses, for the eye has not seen it, and the ear has not heard it, and it does not ordinarily enter the human heart. The more nearly the soul approaches the vision of God, the more it recognizes the invisibility of the divine nature. Sensory impressions and intellectual observations are left behind entirely as the soul pursues its journey to the interior, until its quest takes it to the unseeable and the incomprehensible. There it sees God.

For true knowledge lies in not seeing, for the object of our quest is beyond all knowledge. It is enclosed by a wall of incomprehensibility like a kind of darkness. And that is why the blessed John, who himself penetrated this brilliant darkness, writes that "no one has ever seen God" (Jn 1:18).

Blessed Henry Suso (ca. 1295-1366) was the most famous student of the mystic Meister Eckhart. He was a Dominican mystic and preacher known for *The Book of Eternal Wisdom*.

May All Creation Praise You for Me

∞

My soul has longed for you all night, O eternal wisdom! and in the early morning I turn to you from the depths of my heart. May your holy presence remove all dangers from my soul and body. May your many graces fill the inmost recesses of my heart, and inflame it with your divine love.

O most sweet Jesus! turn your face toward me, for this morning with all the powers of my soul I fly to you and greet you, entreating that the thousand times a thousand angels who minister to you may praise you on my behalf, and that the thousand times ten thousand blessed spirits who surround your throne may glorify you today. May all that is beautiful and lovable in created beings praise you for me, and may all creation bless your holy name, our help and protection in time and in eternity.

St. Hesychius the Priest, the author of *On Watchfulness and Holiness,* was probably an abbot who lived in the eighth or ninth century at Sinai.

Watchfulness
∞

Watchfulness is a spiritual method which, if diligently practiced over a long period, completely frees us with God's help from impassioned thoughts and words and from evil actions. To the extent that this is possible, it leads us to authentic knowledge of the unknowable God, and it helps us penetrate divine and hidden mysteries.

One type of watchfulness is to examine every mental image; for only by means of a mental image can Satan fabricate an evil thought and plant it in the mind in order to lead it astray.

A second type is to silence all thoughts in the heart, and to pray.

A third type is to call, continually and humbly, upon the Lord Jesus Christ for help.

A fourth type is keep the thought of death ever in one's mind.

These types of watchfulness, my child, act like guards and prevent evil thoughts from entering.

St. Hilary of Poitiers (ca. 315-ca. 367) was a married bishop who fought heresy and was exiled by the Emperor Constantius for four years.

Fill My Sails with Wind
∞

The chief service I owe you in my life, as I well know, O God, all-powerful Father, is that every word and thought of mine should speak of you. The power of speech that you gave me can give me no greater pleasure than to serve you by preaching, showing an ignorant world that you are the Father, whose only Son is God.

But in saying this, I am merely saying what I want to do. If I am actually to do it, I must ask you for your help and mercy. Fill with wind the sails I have hoisted for you, and carry me forward on my course. Breathe your Spirit into my faith and the way I confess it. Make it possible for me to continue the preaching I have begun.

St. Hildegard of Bingen (1098-1179), prioress of her religious community, was the first of the great German mystics. A poet, a prophet, and a physician, she did not fear to rebuke popes and princes.

Fire of the Spirit

∞

Fire of the Spirit, life of the lives of creatures,
   spiral of sanctity, bond of all natures,
   glow of charity, lights of clarity,
   taste of sweetness to sinners—
   be with us and hear us.
Composer of all things, light of all the risen,
   key of salvation, release from the dark prison,
   hope of all unions, scope of chastities,
   joy in the glory, strong honor—
   be with us and hear us.

HILDEGARD
OF BINGEN

St. Hippolytus (ca. 170-ca. 236) was a priest in Rome who died in exile because of his faith. He is the author of *The Apostolic Tradition*.

The Sign of the Cross

∞

Imitate Christ at all times, signing your forehead with sincerity. This is the sign of his passion, shown and proven against the devil, if you make it with faith, not in order to be seen by others, but knowingly setting it forward as a shield. For, when the adversary sees that its power comes from the heart, because it shows forth publicly the image of baptism, he is put to flight. He flies, not because of your spittle, but because the Spirit within you blows him away. When Moses made this sign, rubbing the blood of the slain paschal lamb on the lintels of the doorposts, he signified the faith which we now have in the perfect Lamb.

Blessed Humbert of Romans, a Dominican master general, revised liturgy and developed missions in the East in the thirteenth century. This is from his *Treatise on the Formation of Preachers*.

Think Before Speaking
∞

Many people do not think before they speak; whatever comes into their mouth, they utter it without hesitation. This means that they often pour out a stream of idle words. There is an anecdote about this in the *Lives of the Fathers*. Two brothers went to visit St. Anthony, and while they were on their way there they were joined by an old man who wanted to go the same way. While they were in the boat, the two brothers talked a lot of nonsense.

When they arrived at St. Anthony's cell, he asked the old man, "Did you find these brothers good traveling companions?"

He said, "Yes, only their house has no door. Anyone who wants to can go in and untie the ass."

By this he meant that they always uttered any word that came into their mouths. This is the opposite of what is said of the just man, that "his mouth ponders wisdom," which means that he ponders on what he is going to say before he says it. St. Ambrose says, "A word ought to be tested before it is spoken."

St. Ignatius of Antioch (ca. 35-ca. 107) was probably a disciple of St. John the Evangelist. St. Ignatius, who was a bishop in Asia Minor, was thrown to the lions in Rome. This is from a letter he wrote to Christians in Ephesus.

Gather Frequently

Seek to come together more frequently
   to give thanks and glory to God.
For when you gather together frequently,
   the powers of Satan are destroyed,
   and his mischief is brought to nothing
   by the unity of your faith.
There is nothing better than peace,
   by which every war
   in heaven and on earth
   is abolished.

St. Ignatius of Loyola (1491-1556), born to a Spanish noble family, was converted while convalescing from military wounds. He founded the Society of Jesus (Jesuits), originally to be missionaries in Palestine, and developed the *Spiritual Exercises,* a thirty-day guided retreat. His motto was "Find God in all things."

I Give You My Will

∞

*T*ake, Lord, all my liberty.
Receive my memory, my understanding, and my whole will.
Whatever I have and possess, you have given to me;
 to you I restore it completely,
 and to your will I utterly surrender it for your direction.
Give me the grace to love you only,
 and I am rich enough;
 I ask for nothing else.

St. Irenaeus of Lyons (ca. 130-ca. 200) was one of the greatest theologians of the early church. Born in Asia Minor, he became a missionary bishop in Gaul (modern-day France) and author of *Against Heresies,* from which this is taken.

Immortality Is God's Gift
∞

Just as the wooden branch of the vine, placed in the earth, bears fruit in its own time—and as the grain of wheat, falling into the ground and there dissolved, rises with great increase by the Spirit of God, who sustains all things, and then by the wisdom of God serves for the use of men, and when it receives the Word of God becomes the Eucharist, which is the body and blood of Christ—so also our bodies which are nourished by it, and then fall into the earth and are dissolved therein, shall rise at the proper time, the Word of God bestowing on them this rising again, to the glory of God the Father. It is he who indeed grants to this mortal immortality, and gives to the corruptible the gracious gift of incorruption. Our survival forever comes from his greatness, not from our nature.

St. Isaac the Syrian was Bishop of Nineveh late in the seventh century.

The Kingdom Within
∽

Be at peace with your own soul;
  then heaven and earth will be at peace with you.
Enter eagerly into the treasure house that is within you,
  and so you will see the things that are in heaven;
  for there is but one single entry to them both.
The ladder that leads to the kingdom
  is hidden within your soul.
Flee from sin, dive into yourself,
  and in your soul you will discover
  the stairs by which to ascend.

St. Isaiah the Solitary was probably a fifth-century monk who lived first at Sketis in Egypt and then in Palestine. This is from his treatise, "On Guarding the Intellect."

Do Not Leave Your Heart Unguarded

∞

I entreat you not to leave your heart unguarded, so long as you are in the body. Just as a farmer cannot feel confident about the crop growing in his fields, because he does not know what will happen to it before it is stored away in his granary, so a man should not leave his heart unguarded so long as he still has breath in his nostrils. Up to his last breath he cannot know what passion will attack him; so long as he breathes, therefore, he must not leave his heart unguarded, but should at every moment pray to God for His help and mercy.

St. James was known as "the Lord's brother" and "James the Just." He was the first Bishop of Jerusalem and is traditionally considered the author of the New Testament Epistle of James, from which this excerpt is taken (3:13-18). The historian Josephus reports that St. James was stoned to death in A.D. 62.

The Wisdom from Above

W ho is wise and understanding among you? Show by your good life that your works are done with gentleness born of wisdom. But if you have bitter envy and selfish ambition in your hearts, do not be boastful and false to the truth. Such wisdom does not come down from above, but is earthly, unspiritual, devilish. For where there is envy and selfish ambition, there will also be disorder and wickedness of every kind. But the wisdom from above is first pure, then peaceable, gentle, willing to yield, full of mercy and good fruits, without a trace of partiality or hypocrisy. And a harvest of righteousness is sown in peace for those who make peace.

Blessed Jan van Ruysbroeck (1293-1381) was a Flemish mystical writer and contemplative Augustinian canon regular.

The Eternal Sun

When summer draws near and the sun rises higher in the sky, it draws moisture out of the earth through the roots and trunk of a tree into its branches, and as a result leaves, blossoms, and fruit appear. In the same way, when Christ, the eternal sun, rises higher in our hearts and it becomes summer in the rich flowering of virtues, then he sheds his light and heat onto our desires so as to draw the heart from the multiplicity of earthly things to unity and interior fervor. He makes the heart grow and bring forth the leaves of fervent affection, the blossoms of a devotion that is full of desire, and the fruit of thanksgiving and praise, and he preserves this fruit eternally in the humble pain that arises from our constant awareness of our deficiencies.

St. Jerome (ca. 342-420), the greatest biblical scholar of his age, revised and retranslated the Latin Bible, the Vulgate. With his good friend St. Paula he founded a monastery in Bethlehem. This is from a letter Jerome wrote to Nepotianus, a young friend who was becoming a clergyman.

Do Not Listen to Gossip

∞

Beware of a tattling tongue and of itching ears.
Neither gossip about others nor listen to those who do.
It is no excuse to say, "If others tell me things,
   I cannot be rude to them."
No one wants to speak to an unwilling listener.
An arrow never lodges in a stone;
   often it springs back and wounds the one who shot it.
Let the gossip learn from your unwillingness to listen
   to be less ready to hurt others.

St. John was probably the youngest of Jesus' twelve apostles. He is traditionally believed to be the author of the Gospel, the three Epistles that bear his name, and possibly, Revelation. He probably lived until about A.D. 100. This passage is from the beginning of his Gospel (John 1:1-16).

The Word Became Flesh

*I*n the beginning was the Word, and the Word was with God, and the Word was God.... All things came into being through him, and without him not one thing came into being. What has come into being in him was life, and the life was the light of all people. The light shines in the darkness, and the darkness did not overcome it....

He was in the world, and the world came into being through him; yet the world did not know him. He came to what was his own, and his own people did not accept him. But to all who received him, who believed in his name, he gave power to become children of God, who were born, not of blood or of the will of the flesh or of the will of man, but of God.

And the Word became flesh and lived among us, and we have seen his glory, the glory as of a father's only son, full of grace and truth.... From his fullness we have all received, grace upon grace.

St. John Bosco (1815-1888) was a priest, a founder of clubs for girls and boys, and a builder of churches in northern Italy.

Playing Pleases God

∞

A saint was once asked, while playing happily with his companions, what he would do if an angel told him that in a quarter of an hour he would die and appear before the judgment seat of God. The saint promptly replied, "I would continue playing, because I am certain that these games are pleasing to God."

St. John Cassian (ca. 360-ca. 433) lived as a monk in Egypt, Bethlehem, and elsewhere before founding a monastery for monks and another for nuns in Marseilles (present-day France). His books, *Institutes* and *Conferences*, strongly influenced St. Benedict.

Make Haste to Help Me!

"Be pleased, O God, to deliver me.
O Lord, make haste to help me!" (Ps 70:1)

It is not without good reason that this verse has been chosen from the whole of Scripture as a motto. It carries within it all the feelings of which human nature is capable. It can be adapted to every condition and can be usefully deployed against every temptation. It carries within it a cry of help to God in the face of every danger. It expresses the humility of a devout confession. It conveys the watchfulness born of unending worry and fear. It conveys a sense of our frailty, the assurance of being heard, the confidence in help that is always and everywhere present. Someone forever calling out to his protector is indeed very sure of having him close by. This is the voice filled with the ardor of love and of charity. This is the terrified cry of someone who sees the snares of the enemy, the cry of someone besieged day and night and exclaiming that he cannot escape unless his protector comes to the rescue.

81

St. John Chrysostom (ca. 347-407) earned his surname, which means "Golden Mouth," for his eloquent speeches. Archbishop of Constantinople, he was one of the Three Holy Hierarchs of the Eastern church. This is from a sermon called "Dead to Sin."

Sharing in Christ's Resurrection

∞

"Just as Christ was raised from the dead by the glory of the Father, so we too might walk in newness of life" (Rom 6:4). Here Paul tells of the importance of the resurrection.

Do you believe that Christ was raised from the dead? Believe the same of yourself. Just as his death is yours, so also is his resurrection. If you have shared in the one, you shall share in the other. As of now the sin is done away with.

Paul sets before us a demand: to bring about a newness of life by a changing of habits. For when the fornicator becomes chaste, when the covetous person becomes merciful, when the harsh become subdued, a resurrection has taken place, a prelude to the final resurrection which is to come.

How is it a resurrection? It is a resurrection because sin has been mortified, and righteousness has risen in its place; the old life has passed away, and new, angelic life is now being lived.

St. John Climacus (ca. 579-ca. 649), or St. John of the Ladder, was Abbot of Sinai and author of *Ladder to Paradise,* a mystical book popular in both East and West during the Middle Ages.

Laughter in Our Soul

∞

God does not insist or desire that we should mourn in agony of heart; rather, it is his wish that out of love for him we should rejoice with laughter in our soul. Take away sin, and tears become superfluous; where there is no bruise, no ointment is required. Before the fall Adam shed no tears, and in the same way there will be no more tears after the resurrection from the dead, when sin has been destroyed. For pain, sorrow, and lamentation will then have fled away.

St. John Vianney (1786-1859) was a humble curate in Ars, a small village near Lyons, France. Known for his gifts of healing and spiritual discernment, he was visited by over one hundred thousand pilgrims in just the year before his death.

No Middle Path

∞

*W*e must never lose sight of the fact
    that we are either saints or outcasts,
    that we must live for heaven or for hell:
    there is no middle path in this.
You either belong wholly to the world
    or wholly to God.
If people would do for God what they do for the world,
    what a great number of Christians would go to heaven.

St. John of Karpathos was probably a seventh-century monk and bishop from an island between Crete and Rhodes. He wrote to encourage monks in India, or perhaps Ethiopia.

Blessed Are Those Who Endure

∞

It may happen that for a certain time a man is illumined and refreshed by God's grace, and then this grace is withdrawn. This makes him inwardly confused and he starts to grumble; instead of seeking through steadfast prayer to recover his assurance of salvation, he loses patience and gives up. He is like a beggar who receives alms from the palace, and feels put out because he was not asked inside to dine with the king. "Blessed are those who have not seen and yet have come to believe" (Jn 20:29). Blessed also are those who, when grace is withdrawn, find no consolation in themselves, but only continuing tribulation and thick darkness, and yet do not despair; but, strengthened by faith, they endure courageously, convinced that they do indeed see him who is invisible.

St. John of the Cross (1542-1591) was the author of such mystical classics as *The Ascent of Mount Carmel* and *The Dark Night of the Soul.* He helped St. Teresa of Avila found the Discalced Carmelites. This passage comes from *Living Flame of Love.*

God Is Seeking You
∞

If you are seeking after God, you may be sure of this: God is seeking you much more. He is the Lover, and you are his beloved. He has promised himself to you.

In every quiet longing, you call him. With even your inmost prayer, you ask him to come near to you. Your true heart's desire is what attracts him, like a fragrance rising on the air. But in your thoughts, you wonder if he hears you at all. You must see the truth about this matter.

The longing in your soul is actually his doing. You may feel only the smallest desire for him. There may be no emotion about it at all. But the reason your desire rises at all is because he is passing very near to you. His holy beauty comes near you, like a spiritual scent, and it stirs your drowsing soul.

I tell you again—it is not of your doing at all, this moment when your soul awakens. He creates in you the desire to find him and run after him—to follow wherever he leads you, and to press peacefully against his heart wherever he is.

86

St. John the Baptist was Jesus' cousin, sent to "prepare the way of the Lord" (Is 40:3; Mt 3:3). John's forthright preaching attracted large crowds but angered Herod, who imprisoned St. John and later beheaded him. This description of him is from the third chapter of St. Luke's Gospel (Lk 3:7-14).

What, Then, Should We Do?

John said to the crowds that came out to be baptized by him, "You brood of vipers! Who warned you to flee from the wrath to come? Bear fruits worthy of repentance. Do not begin to say to yourselves, 'We have Abraham as our ancestor'; for I tell you, God is able from these stones to raise up children to Abraham. Even now the ax is lying at the root of the trees; every tree therefore that does not bear good fruit is cut down and thrown into the fire."

And the crowds asked him, "What then should we do?" In reply he said to them, "Whoever has two coats must share with anyone who has none; and whoever has food must do likewise." Even tax collectors came to be baptized, and they asked him, "Teacher, what should we do?" He said to them, "Collect no more than the amount prescribed for you." Soldiers also asked him, "And we, what should we do?" He said to them, "Do not extort money from anyone by threats or false accusation, and be satisfied with your wages."

St. Joseph was the husband of Mary and foster-father of Jesus. A carpenter by trade, he probably died before Jesus began his ministry. He is the patron saint of workers. This is St. Matthew's account (Mt 1:18-24).

An Angel Explains

∞

Now the birth of Jesus the Messiah took place in this way. When his mother Mary had been engaged to Joseph, but before they lived together, she was found to be with child from the Holy Spirit. Her husband Joseph, being a righteous man and unwilling to expose her to public disgrace, planned to dismiss her quietly.

But just when he had resolved to do this, an angel of the Lord appeared to him in a dream and said, "Joseph, son of David, do not be afraid to take Mary as your wife, for the child conceived in her is from the Holy Spirit. She will bear a son, and you are to name him Jesus, for he will save his people from their sins."

All this took place to fulfill what had been spoken by the Lord through the prophet:

"Look, the virgin shall conceive and bear a son, and they shall name him Emmanuel," which means, "God is with us."

When Joseph awoke from sleep, he did as the angel of the Lord commanded him.

Blessed Jordan of Saxony, the second master general of the Dominicans, was an eloquent preacher. He drowned on his way to Palestine in 1237. He wrote this advice in an encyclical letter in 1233.

A Challenge to Live Fruitfully

∞

*H*appy are those who keep to the golden mean, giving everything its proper measure; who avoid both cowardice and impetuousness so that they can help plenty of other people without losing their own most useful practice of self-knowledge and constant, watchful, self-criticism; who do whatever they do, not because they are driven by the wind of human approval, but because charity urges them on and the Spirit of God constrains them; who let nothing of what they do or say fall fruitless to the ground, and whose path is not aimless. In everything they look purely and simply to the glory of God, the spiritual benefit of their neighbor, or their own salvation.

My dearest friends, rejoice if you are such as these, and seek to abound still more. But if you are not yet like this, work at it, devote energy and attention to it, so that you may grow toward salvation in the One who called you to this state of grace in which you find yourself.

Blessed Julian of Norwich (ca. 1342-ca. 1420) was a female recluse known only by the name of the church where she lived, the Church of St. Edmund and St. Julian in Norwich, England. At the age of thirty she had sixteen "showings" or mystical visions, which she described in *Revelations of Divine Love.*

Creator, Lover, Protector

Our Lord showed me a spiritual sight of his homely and familiar love. He showed me a little thing, the size of a hazelnut, lying in the palm of my hand, as round as a ball. I looked at it and thought, "What can this be?" And I was answered, "It is all that is made." I wondered how it could last, for I thought that being so small it might suddenly fall apart. And I was answered in my understanding, "It lasts, and always will, because God loves it." And so everything has its being through the love of God.

In this little thing I saw three properties. The first is that God made it; the second is that God loves it; the third is that God preserves it. But what is that to me? It is that God is the creator, the lover, and the protector. For until I am united to him I cannot know love or rest or true happiness; that is, until I am so at one with him that no created thing can come between my God and me.

Blessed Junípero Serra (1713-1784) was a Spanish Franciscan known for his missionary work among Native Americans of Texas, Mexico, and California.

No Capital Punishment
∞

It is indeed right that the soldiers guard and accompany the missionary, but if despite this the Indians should kill a missionary, what good will we achieve by going to war against them? The military will answer me by saying: "We will inflict an exemplary punishment on them so that they will not kill others." To this I reply: "Allow the murderer to live so that he can be saved." This is our purpose here. The murderer should be told, after some moderate punishment, that he is forgiven. Thus we shall fulfill our Christian law, which commands us to forgive injury and to seek not the sinner's death, but his eternal salvation.

St. Justin was a philosopher who converted to Christianity and became one of its foremost defenders. He is often called Justin Martyr because he was beheaded for his faith in about 165. This is from his *First Apology*.

Nourished by Christ's Body and Blood
∞

When the president has given thanks and the whole congregation has assented, those whom we call deacons give to each of those present a portion of the consecrated bread and wine and water, and they take it to the absent. This food we call Eucharist, of which no one is allowed to partake except one who believes that the things we teach are true, and has received the washing for forgiveness of sins and for rebirth, and who lives as Christ handed down to us. For we do not receive these things as common bread or common drink; but as Jesus Christ our Saviour being incarnate by God's word took flesh and blood for our salvation, so also we have been taught that the food consecrated by the word of prayer which comes from him, from which our flesh and blood are nourished by transformation, is the flesh and blood of that incarnate Jesus.

St. Katherine of Alexandria is not on the official saints' list today because nothing is known for sure about her. Nevertheless, over sixty medieval English churches were dedicated to this reputed fourth-century martyr. Writings have been attributed to her, and she was a favorite of St. Catherine of Siena.

All My Learning
∞

All who are descended from Adam and Eve would be destroyed, if God's goodness were not greater—he who loved us so much, though we behaved so badly, that he took blood and bone from a maiden's body. He showed us his face, and walked, while it was his will, among worldly people; and when he had freed us from the enemy's chains, went up as he wished to live where he lives forever without limit.

So we know well, through the wonders that he worked which no human could do, that he is true God; and again, through his suffering and death on the cross as a mortal, that he is also truly human: from his Father, truly God, from his mother, truly human, both together in unity—true human and true God, ruling and guiding all worldly things according to his will.

This is my Lord in whom I believe. This is all the learning I now learn.

St. Leander of Seville was the bishop responsible for the Synods of Toledo and Seville in Spain in the late sixth century. He was a friend of St. Gregory the Great. Here is his advice to a woman responsible for training young nuns.

Do Not Criticize the Absent
∞

*I*t is a great sin against God to criticize a person who is absent and to run down someone else's character. There is no love in doing this. To the contrary, ill will is obvious. The loving action is to correct someone to her face rather than to tear her apart behind her back.

If a damaging report has reached your ears about some sister, sigh as if you were grieving over your own sins. And since "we are all one in Christ," be compassionate to her as if to a member of your own body. Try to heal the ill member, not to amputate it. Correct her gently in your presence, that she may be cured. Do not criticize her behind her back, or you will sin and further wound someone who is already wounded.

Guard your heart with all care, so that you do not listen to complaining and grow accustomed to it. For she whom you criticize is your own member; she is the body of Christ.

St. Leontius of Cyprus, a Greek Father of the sixth and seventh centuries, defended the liturgical use of icons—stylized paintings of Christ, the Blessed Virgin Mary, or a saint.

Through Me All Creations Worships
∝

*T*hrough sky and earth and sea,
 through wood and stone,
 through all creation visible and invisible,
 I offer worship to the Creator and Master and
 Maker of all things.
For the creation does not worship the Maker
 directly and by itself,
 but through me the heavens declare the glory of God,
 through me the moon worships God,
 through me the stars glorify God,
 through me the waters and showers of rain,
 the dews and all creation,
 worship God and give him glory.

St. Macarius of Egypt lived during the fourth century as a hermit in the desert of Skete.

To You I Hasten

To you, O Master who loves all humankind,
    I hasten on rising from sleep.
By your mercy I go out to do your work,
    and I make my prayer to you.
Help me at all times and in all things.
Deliver me from every evil thing of this world
    and from pursuit by the devil.
Save me and bring me to your eternal kingdom.
For you are my Creator;
    you inspire all good thoughts in me.
In you is all my hope,
    and to you I give glory, now and for ever.

St. Makarii of Optino (1788-1860) was a Russian *starets*—an elder who offers spiritual guidance and healing.

The Broom of Humility
∞

*P*ray simply. Do not expect to find in your heart any remarkable gift of prayer. Consider yourself unworthy of it. Then you will find peace.

Use the empty, cold dryness of your prayer as food for your humility. Repeat constantly: I am not worthy, Lord, I am not worthy! But say it calmly, without agitation. This humble prayer will be acceptable to God.

Remember that the most important thing of all is humility. Remember, too, that Isaac the Syrian warns us that God's wrath visits all who refuse the bitter cross of agony, the cross of active suffering, and who, striving after visions and special graces of prayer, waywardly seek to appropriate the glories of the Cross.

He also says, "God's grace comes of itself, suddenly, without our seeing it approach. It comes when the place is clean." Therefore, carefully, diligently, constantly clean the place; sweep it with the broom of humility.

Blessed Marie of the Incarnation, a married woman with children, brought the Discalced Carmelites to France in 1604 and served as an unofficial novice mistress for them.

Union with God

∞

My will had been completely moved and was now plunged into an encompassing union, which lasted until the end of my prayer. The subject of my meditation was this:

Since God is love,

    I should also be all love in this union.

Since God is fire,

    being in him I should burn and become fire like him.

Since love is the bond of perfection,

    I should want no other bond.

Following these transports, I found myself in a state of great detachment from all creatures and in a perfect disposition to cling to my heavenly spouse everywhere and at all times. If he wished me to go to the ends of the earth, this would become my country. Because he is everywhere, all places are the same for me.

St. Mark the Ascetic probably lived as a desert hermit in Palestine or Egypt during the fifth century. He was also superior of a religious community in Asia Minor. This is from a letter he wrote to another hermit, Nicolas.

Remember God's Blessings

∞

Do not let yourself be dragged down unwittingly by vice and laziness, so that you forget the gifts you have received through God's love. Bring before your eyes the blessings, whether physical or spiritual, conferred on you from the beginning of your life down to the present, and call them repeatedly to mind in accordance with the words: "Do not forget all his benefits" (Ps 103:2). Then your heart will readily be moved to the fear and love of God, so that you repay him, as far as you can, by your strict life, virtuous conduct, devout conscience, wise speech, true faith, and humility—in short, by dedicating your whole self to God. When you are moved by the recollection of all these blessings which you have received through God's loving goodness, your heart will be spontaneously wounded with longing and love; for he has not done for others who are much better than yourself such miraculous things as in his ineffable love he has done for you.

St. Martin of Braga was a sixth-century bishop and missionary in Spain.

Overlook Injuries

∞

*I*f you do not wish to become angry, do not be curious. If you ask what is being said about yourself and uncover unpleasant words (even though these words were said privately), you only make yourself unhappy.

Those who are wise overlook many wrongs and often do not take them as such, for either they do not know about them or, if they do, they make fun of them and turn them into jokes. To pay no attention to injuries is a mark of magnanimity. The really great and noble soul listens to wrongs as securely as the larger wild animals hear the barking of small dogs.

The Blessed Virgin Mary, the mother of Jesus, is preeminent among the communion of saints. Mary sang the Magnificat (Lk 1:46-55) while visiting her cousin St. Elizabeth, soon to be mother of St. John the Baptist.

Magnificat
∞

My soul magnifies the Lord,
   and my spirit rejoices in God my Savior,
      for he has looked with favor on the lowliness of his servant.
Surely, from now on all generations will call me blessed;
   for the Mighty One has done great things for me,
   and holy is his name.
His mercy is for those who fear him
   from generation to generation....
He has brought down the powerful from their thrones,
   and lifted up the lowly;
   he has filled the hungry with good things,
   and sent the rich away empty.
He has helped his servant Israel,
   in remembrance of his mercy,
      according to the promise he made to our ancestors,
      to Abraham and to his descendants forever.

St. Mary and St. Martha were sisters of St. Lazarus, whom Jesus raised from the dead. Jesus enjoyed spending time with the three of them in their home in Bethany, a suburb of Jerusalem. Their story is told in Luke 10:38-42.

Only One Thing Is Needed

∞

Jesus entered a certain village, where a woman named Martha welcomed him into her home. She had a sister named Mary, who sat at the Lord's feet and listened to what he was saying. But Martha was distracted by her many tasks; so she came to him and asked, "Lord, do you not care that my sister has left me to do all the work by myself? Tell her then to help me."

But the Lord answered her, "Martha, Martha, you are worried and distracted by many things; there is need of only one thing. Mary has chosen the better part, which will not be taken away from her."

St. Mary Magdalene was one of Jesus' closest friends. He healed her of demon possession, and she became one of his followers. One of the first witnesses of the risen Lord, she was sent by him to announce his resurrection to the disciples. Their encounter is described in John 20:11-18.

I Have Seen the Lord

∞

Mary stood weeping outside the tomb. As she wept, she bent over to look into the tomb; and she saw two angels in white, sitting where the body of Jesus had been lying. They said to her, "Woman, why are you weeping?"

She said to them, "They have taken away my Lord, and I do not know where they have laid him."

When she had said this, she turned around and saw Jesus standing there, but she did not know that it was Jesus. Jesus said to her, "Woman, why are you weeping? Whom are you looking for?"

Supposing him to be the gardener, she said to him, "Sir, if you have carried him away, tell me where you have laid him, and I will take him away."

Jesus said to her, "Mary!"

She turned and said to him in Hebrew, "Rabbouni!" (which means Teacher).

Jesus said to her, "Do not hold on to me, because I have not yet ascended to the Father. But go to my brothers and say to them, 'I am ascending to my Father and your Father, to my God and your God.'"

Mary Magdalene went and announced to the disciples, "I have seen the Lord."

St. Mary Magdalene dei Pazzi (1566-1607), from an illustrious Florentine family, became a Carmelite at age sixteen. She suffered disease and spiritual assaults, but she also enjoyed extraordinary spiritual graces.

Treasures of the Spirit

∞

Holy Spirit, Spirit of truth,
you are the reward of the saints,
the comforter of souls,
light in the darkness,
riches to the poor,
wealth to lovers,
food for the hungry,
hospitality to wanderers.
You are the one in whom
all treasures are contained.

St. Matthew was a tax collector, and undoubtedly a swindler, when Jesus called him to be one of the twelve disciples. Author of the Gospel of Matthew, he wrote this account of that turning point in his life. It is found in chapter 9:9-13.

Not the Righteous, but Sinners
∞

As Jesus was walking along, he saw a man called Matthew sitting at the tax booth; and he said to him, "Follow me." And he got up and followed him.

And as he sat at dinner in the house, many tax collectors and sinners came and were sitting with him and his disciples. When the Pharisees saw this, they said to his disciples, "Why does your teacher eat with tax collectors and sinners?"

But when he heard this, he said, "Those who are well have no need of a physician, but those who are sick…. For I have come to call not the righteous but sinners."

St. Maximus the Confessor (ca. 580-662) was an abbot, a theologian, and a fighter of heresies, remembered today as one of the fathers of Eastern mysticism.

The Mirror of Creation
∽

We do not know God in his essence. We know him rather from the grandeur of his creation and from his providential care for all creatures. For by this means, as if using a mirror, we attain insight into his infinite goodness, wisdom, and power.

St. Mechthildis of Magdeburg (1212-ca. 1282)

was a nun at the convent of Helfta and novice-mistress of St. Gertrude the Great, also a famous mystic. St. Mechthild described her visions and religious experience in *Flowing Light of the Divinity*.

Let Me Be True to You

*L*ord, you have taken away from me everything
    I once had of you.
Nevertheless, by your grace, please leave me one gift—
    a gift every dog has by nature.
Please let me be true to you in my distress,
    even though I no longer feel your presence.
This I desire more fervently than anything else
    in your heavenly kingdom.

St. Melito of Sardis was a bishop in Asia Minor during the second century.

A Hymn to Jesus Christ

∽

It is the Lord who made heaven and earth,
   who in the beginning formed humanity,
   who was announced by law and prophets,
   who was incarnate in a virgin,
   who was suspended from the wood.
Buried in the earth,
   he was raised from the dead
   and ascended into the heights
   and is now seated at the right hand of the Father
   and has the power to judge and the power to save all.
Through him the Father made
   that which has been made from the beginning
   and even unto ages unending:
   Alpha and Omega, beginning and end—
   beginning inexpressible, ending incomprehensible—
   Christ, King, Jesus, Captain, Lord,
   risen from the dead, sitting at the right hand of the Father—
   in the Father, the Father in him—
   to him be glory and power forever.

St. Neilos the Ascetic, who died about 430, was abbot of a monastery near Ankara in present-day Turkey. He was one of the first to refer explicitly to the Jesus Prayer, a short meditation used especially in the Eastern churches. This is from the closing of *Ascetic Discourse.*

God's Judgments Are True

∾

From malice humans often speak slanderously of what is good; but the tribunal on high gives judgment with impartiality, and delivers its verdict in accordance with the truth.

Let us, then, bring joy to this heavenly tribunal, which rejoices in our acts of righteousness. We need not worry about human opinions, for humans can neither reward those who have lived well nor punish those who have lived otherwise. If because of envy or worldly attachment they seek to discredit the way of holiness, they are defaming with deluded blasphemies the life honored by God and the angels. At the time of judgment those who have lived rightly will be rewarded with eternal blessings, not on the basis of human opinion, but in accordance with the true nature of their life.

May all of us attain these blessings through the grace and love of our Lord Jesus Christ, to whom be glory together with the Father and the Holy Spirit, now and ever and through all the ages. Amen.

St. Nicodemos of the Holy Mountain

(1749-1809), an Orthodox monk and scholar, compiled the five-volume *Philokalia*, a collection of ancient writings on the spiritual life.

Delight in God's Word

∞

A source of spiritual delight is the Word of God contained in Holy Scripture. In Scripture is found the ultimate truth that enlightens the mind, which, as mind, has truth as its object. Moreover, there is intense sweetness and grace in the words of Scripture, which draw like a great magnet the hearts of the readers to agree with them and to be persuaded. This is only natural. After all, the words of Scripture are the words of God and of the Holy Spirit. That is to say, they are the words of truth itself and grace itself.

St. Pachomius (ca. 292-348) was the Egyptian founder of Christian communal monasticism. During his lifetime some nine thousand monks and nuns in several monasteries followed his rule, which later influenced St. Benedict's.

Care Nothing for Praise
∞

I urge you from my heart to care nothing for praise. Vanity is the devil's own weapon. This was how Eve was tricked: he told her, "Eat the fruit of the tree; your eyes will open and you will be like gods." She listened, thinking it was true. She ran after the divine glory and her very humanity was taken away. If you, too, seek praise it will make you a stranger to God's glory. In Eve's case, no one wrote her to warn her before she was tempted by the devil. But you have been warned in the Holy Scriptures and by the saints who have gone ahead of you. Therefore do not say, I have never heard of all this. For it is written, "Their voice goes out through all the earth, and their words to the end of the world" (Ps 19:4).

Now then, if you are praised, control your feelings and give glory to God. If you are cursed, give glory to God and thank him that you have been allowed to share the lot of his Son and of his saints.

St. Patrick (ca. 389–ca. 461) is the patron saint and legendary apostle of Ireland. Son of an English deacon and grandson of a priest, he was kidnapped and taken to Ireland as a slave. He escaped after a few years, became a priest, and returned to Ireland as a missionary bishop. This is from a prayer called St. Patrick's Breastplate.

I Rise Today

∞

I rise today
    in heaven's might,
    in sun's brightness,
    in moon's radiance,
    in fire's glory,
    in lightning's quickness,
    in wind's swiftness,
    in sea's depth,
    in earth's stability,
    in rock's fixity.
I rise today
    in power's strength, invoking the Trinity,
    believing in threeness,
    confessing the oneness,
    of creation's Creator.

St. Paul (ca. 5-ca. 67), known as the Apostle to the Gentiles, was the author of many New Testament letters. He was also a Pharisee with a solid rabbinic education. At first an opponent of Christianity, he was dramatically converted to the new movement in about the year 35. He became the early church's greatest missionary and most influential theologian. This is from his longest book, The Epistle to the Romans (Rom 8:31-35, 37-39).

Nothing Can Separate Us from God's Love
∽

*I*f God is for us, who is against us? He who did not withhold his own Son, but gave him up for all of us, will he not with him also give us everything else? Who will bring any charge against God's elect? It is God who justifies. Who is to condemn? It is Christ Jesus, who died, yes, who was raised, who is at the right hand of God, who indeed intercedes for us. Who will separate us from the love of Christ? Will hardship, or distress, or persecution, or famine, or nakedness, or peril, or sword?… No, in all these things we are more than conquerors through him who loved us. For I am convinced that neither death, nor life, nor angels, nor rulers, nor things present, nor things to come, nor powers, nor height, nor depth, nor anything else in all creation, will be able to separate us from the love of God in Christ Jesus our Lord.

St. Paulinus of Nola (ca. 354-431) was born into a wealthy French family. Thanks to his Spanish wife, he converted to Christianity. At the age of forty, he became a priest in Italy; fifteen years later, he was made a bishop.

We Believe in the Resurrection

∞

We do not guess at what the afterlife holds. We do not base our faith on human opinions, poets' dreams, or philosophers' images. We draw our faith from the very fountain of truth, God himself. And who could have greater knowledge of divine things?

We do not teach that souls pass into other bodies so that humans become animals, or that souls live on without bodies, or that souls die in the body. We don't need these lies, because we have Truth itself. This Truth—God and his Word—has promised in its teaching and proved in its rising again that the flesh will be raised to eternal life. Since we have these proofs and the light of faith, how could we ever doubt the resurrection, which we have heard from God's Word and seen and felt with the eyes and hands of the apostles?

St. Peter Canisius (1521-1597) was a Jesuit who worked to rebuild the Catholic Church in the years immediately following the Reformation.

A Time for Mercy

∞

O God,
  the shelter of the poor,
  the strength of the exhausted,
  and the comforter of the grieving,
  we entrust to your mercy the unfortunate and needy
  wherever they may be.
You alone know how long and how much
  they have suffered.
Look down, Father of mercies,
  at those unhappy families suffering from war and violence,
  from hunger and disease,
  and other cruel trials.
Spare them, O Lord,
  for it is truly a time for mercy.

St. Peter was a leader among the twelve disciples and is traditionally regarded as the first pope. A fisherman by trade, Peter left his nets after the resurrection and traveled, with his wife, throughout Asia Minor, preaching the gospel of the risen Christ. According to an ancient tradition, he was crucified upside down in Rome in about A.D. 67 and is buried under the high altar of St. Peter's Basilica in the Vatican. Here is Peter's testimony as recorded in 2 Peter 1:16-19.

A Lamp Before Dawn

We did not follow cleverly devised myths when we made known to you the power and coming of our Lord Jesus Christ, but we had been eyewitnesses of his majesty. For he received honor and glory from God the Father when that voice was conveyed to him by the Majestic Glory, saying, "This is my Son, my Beloved, with whom I am well pleased." We ourselves heard this voice come from heaven, while we were with him on the holy mountain.

So we have the prophetic message more fully confirmed. You will do well to be attentive to this as to a lamp shining in a dark place, until the day dawns and the morning star rises in your hearts.

St. Photina is the name given by some Eastern churches to the woman at the well, whom Jesus sent to announce the good news to the Samaritans. According to legend, she was one of a group of martyrs in Rome. Her story is told in the fourth chapter of the Gospel of John (Jn 4:27-30, 39-41).

Come and See!

∞

*J*esus' disciples... were astonished that he was speaking with a woman, but no one said,... "Why are you speaking with her?"

Then the woman left her water jar and went back to the city. She said to the people, "Come and see a man who told me everything I have ever done! He cannot be the Messiah, can he?"

Many Samaritans from that city believed in him because of the woman's testimony, "He told me everything I have ever done." So when the Samaritans came to him, they asked him to stay with them; and he stayed there two days. And many more believed because of his word. They said to the woman, "It is no longer because of what you said that we believe, for we have heard for ourselves, and we know that this is truly the Savior of the world."

St. Polycarp (ca. 69–ca. 155), a disciple of St. John, was Bishop of Smyrna, now Izmir in western Turkey. At the age of eighty-six he was burned at the stake for refusing to worship the emperor. This is a letter he wrote to the Christians in Philippi.

The Character of Leaders

∞

Church leaders must be compassionate and merciful to all. They must bring back those who have strayed. They must care for all who are weak, and they must not neglect widows or orphans or poor people. They must refrain from all anger, favoritism, and unjust judgment. They must not be greedy or grasping. They must not quickly believe evil of anyone or jump to conclusions, for we all owe the debt of sin.

St. Priscilla was a Jewish convert to Christianity and wife of St. Aquila. Priscilla and Aquila traveled with St. Paul, taught theology to the Alexandrian preacher Apollos, and hosted a house church. In the controversial opinion of one influential Scripture scholar, Priscilla may have been the author of the Epistle to the Hebrews, from which this is taken (12:7-13).

For Our Own Good

∞

Endure trials for the sake of discipline. God is treating you as children; for what child is there whom a parent does not discipline? If you do not have that discipline in which all children share, then you are illegitimate and not his children. Moreover, we had human parents to discipline us, and we respected them. Should we not be even more willing to be subject to the Father of spirits and live? For they disciplined us for a short time as seemed best to them, but he disciplines us for our good, in order that we may share his holiness. Now, discipline always seems painful rather than pleasant at the time, but later it yields the peaceful fruit of righteousness to those who have been trained by it.

Therefore lift your drooping hands and strengthen your weak knees, and make straight paths for your feet, so that what is lame may not be put out of joint, but rather be healed.

St. Proclus was Patriarch of Constantinople and an influential theologian known for his gentleness amidst controversy. He died in 446. This is from one of his sermons.

God in a Womb

∞

Who ever saw, who ever heard of the infinite God dwelling in a womb? Heaven is not large enough for him, yet a womb was not too small for him. He was born of woman—this God who is not only God, this man who is not merely man. His birth changed the doorway to sin into the gate of salvation. Through Eve's disobedient ears the serpent injected poison; through Mary's obedient ears the Word entered to form a living temple. The merciful God was not shamed by a woman's pains, for through them life was born. A woman's pains were the beginning of our salvation. Had God not been born of a woman, he would not have died. Had he not died, he would not have destroyed, through death, "the one who has the power of death, that is, the devil" (Heb 2:14). Had the Word not dwelt in a womb, the flesh would never have sat on the throne.

Blessed Richard Rolle (ca. 1300-1349) was an English hermit known for his mystical writings. This prayer is from *The Fire of Love*.

No Sweeter Delight

∞

O lovely Eternal Love, that raised us from the depths and showed us the wonder of your divine Majesty. Come to me, my Love! I gave up all I had for you. I shunned all that might have been mine, so that my soul might be a home and source of comfort for you. Do not forsake me when you know I am glowing with desire for you; when you know that my most burning desire is to be embraced by you. Give me grace to love you and to rest in you, that in your kingdom I may be worthy of seeing you without end.

I know of no sweeter delight than to sing to you and praise you in my heart, Jesus my love. I know of no greater or more plenteous joy than to feel the sweet heat of love in my mind. Come, my Saviour, and comfort my soul; make me constant in my love, that I may never cease to love you.

St. Richard of Chichester (ca. 1197-1253), a bishop and a chancellor of Oxford University, was noted for his generosity as well as for his reforms.

Day by Day
∞

We thank you, Lord Jesus Christ,
   for all the blessings you have won for us,
   for all the pains and insults you have endured for us.
O most merciful Redeemer, Friend, and Brother,
   may we know you more clearly,
   love you more dearly,
   and follow you more nearly day by day.

St. Robert Bellarmine (1542-1621), a Jesuit, was known for his learning. He taught at Louvain and Rome, was a cardinal and an archbishop, and was head of the Vatican Library.

Nobody is Perfect
∞

$\mathcal{P}$eace and union are the most necessary of all things for people who live or work together. Nothing serves so well to establish and maintain them as the patient love that allows us to put up with the faults of others. Nobody is perfect. We are all in some way burdens to others, whether we are bosses or workers, old or young, academics or illiterates.

St. Saturus was one of the companions of the young mothers, St. Perpetua and St. Felicity, who were martyred in North Africa in A.D. 203. This is his account of a vision he had just before his death.

A Vision of Heaven
∞

We had died, and four angels began to carry us eastward. When we were beyond the world, we first saw an intense light. Then a great open space appeared. It seemed to be a garden with rose bushes and all kinds of flowers. The trees were tall as cypresses, and their leaves were constantly falling. In the garden were four other angels. When they saw us, they greeted us with respect and said: "Here they are! Here they are!"

Then we came to a place whose walls seemed to be made of light. In front of the gate stood four angels, who went through the gate and put on white robes. We also entered, and we heard the sound of voices chanting endlessly in unison, "Holy, holy, holy!"

In the same place we saw an aged man with white hair and a youthful face. On his right and left were four elders. Surprised, we went toward him and stood before a throne. Four angels lifted us up; we kissed the aged man, and he touched our faces with his hand. Then the elders said to us, "Go and play."

St. Seraphim of Sarov (1759-1833) was a
Russian monk and spiritual director.

Joy in the Holy Spirit
∞

When the Spirit of God descends upon you
  and overshadows you with the fullness of his outpouring,
  then your soul overflows with indescribable joy,
  for the Holy Spirit turns to joy whatever he touches.
The reign of heaven is peace and joy in the Holy Spirit.
Acquire inward peace,
  and thousands around you will find their salvation.

St. Serapion of Thmuis was a fourth-century
Egyptian bishop who edited an important collection
of early liturgical texts.

A Prayer for Life and Light

*W*e praise you, Father, invisible, giver of immortality.
You are the source of life and light, grace and truth.
You love men and women, and you love the poor.
You seek reconciliation with us,
   and you draw us to you by sending your dear Son to us.
We beg you, give us true life;
   give us the spirit of light,
   that we may know you, the highest truth,
   and the one you sent, Jesus Christ.
Give us the Holy Spirit
   and let us speak openly of your indescribable mysteries.
May the Lord Jesus and the Holy Spirit speak in us
   and praise you through us,
   for you are high above all earthly and heavenly powers,
   above everything that can be named
   in this world and in the world to come.

St. Symeon the New Theologian (949-1022) was a Greek ascetic and mystic.

I in God, and God in Me

I know that the Immovable comes down;
  I know that the Invisible appears to me;
  I know that he who is far outside the whole creation
  takes me within himself and hides me in his arms,
  and then I find myself outside the whole world.
I, a frail, small mortal in the world,
  behold the Creator of the world,
  all of him, within myself;
  and I know that I shall not die,
  for I am within the Life,
  I have the whole of Life springing up as a fountain within me.
He is in my heart, he is in heaven:
  both there and here
  he shows himself to me with equal glory.

St. Teresa of Avila (1515-1582), one of two female Doctors of the Church, was both a mystic and an activist. With St. John of the Cross she founded the Discalced Carmelites. Her writings include *The Way of Perfection* and *The Interior Castle*, from which this is taken.

Advice to Beginners in Prayer
∞

As we begin the practice of prayer, we must not become content with the consolations we may receive at the early stages. That would be like building our house on sand. At this stage you are beginning to build a beautiful castle, and you must build it on strong virtues, not temporary consolations.

Neither should we complain about a lack of consolations at this stage. Rather, embrace the cross that Jesus bore upon his shoulders and realize that this cross is yours to carry too. We are free to the extent that we are able to suffer....

All that beginners in prayer must do is this: labor and be resolute, preparing themselves with diligence to bring their will into conformity with God's will. This ability is the greatest thing that can be accomplished on the spiritual journey.

TERESA

OF AVILA

St. Theodore of Studios (759-826) was the abbott of a monastery in Constantinople. Under his leadership, it became one of the greatest in the world.

How Splendid the Cross

∽

How splendid the cross of Christ!
It brings life, not death;
   light, not darkness;
   Paradise, not its loss.
It is the wood on which
   the Lord, like a great warrior,
   was wounded in hands and feet and side,
   but healed thereby our wounds.
A tree had destroyed us;
   a tree now brought us life.

St. Theophane the Recluse (1815-1894) was a Russian priest, theologian, missionary, bishop, and abbot before retiring from public life and becoming a hermit. While a recluse, he continued to write—theological books as well as ten volumes of letters.

The Christian Life

∞

*T*here comes a distinct moment when a person begins to live as a Christian. At this moment, the identifying marks of the Christian life appear in the person.

The Christian life is marked by zeal. It is a life of constant communion with God, a life of actively doing God's holy will. We live this life by faith in our Lord Jesus Christ, with the help of God's grace, to the glory of his most holy name.

Though the essence of Christian life is communion with God in Christ Jesus our Lord, at first this communion is hidden from others and also from ourselves. The visible or tangible witness that we are living the Christian life is our zeal to please God alone. In our ardor we sacrifice ourselves and hate everything opposed to God's will.

And so, when our ardent zeal begins, we know that Christian life has begun; and when zeal is constantly at work in our lives, we know we are living the Christian life.

St. Thérèse of Lisieux (1873-1897), called the Little Flower, was a French Carmelite nun. Ordered to write her autobiography, she became world-famous after her death from tuberculosis at age twenty-four. Mother Teresa of Calcutta was so inspired by her writings that she adopted her name.

The Power of Prayer
∞

The power of prayer is really tremendous. It makes one like a queen who can approach the king at any time and get whatever she asks for. To be sure of an answer, there is no need to recite from a book a formula composed for the occasion. If there were, I should have to be pitied.

Though I'm quite unworthy, I love to say the Divine Office every day, but apart from that I cannot bring myself to hunt through books for beautiful prayers. There are so many of them that I get a headache. Besides, each prayer seems lovelier than the next. I cannot possibly say them all and do not know which to choose. I behave like children who cannot read: I tell God very simply what I want, and he always understands.

For me, prayer is an upward leap of the heart, an untroubled glance toward heaven, a cry of gratitude and love which I utter from the depths of sorrow as well as from the heights of joy. It has a supernatural grandeur that expands the soul and unites it with God.

St. Thomas, one of the twelve apostles, is remembered for his doubt and subsequent belief. Tradition says that he was a missionary to Southern India. The story is from the Gospel of John (Jn 20:24-29).

Seeing and Believing

∞

*T*homas… was not with [the other disciples] when Jesus came. So the other disciples told him, "We have seen the Lord."

But he said to them, "Unless I see the mark of the nails in his hands, and put my finger in the mark of the nails and my hand in his side, I will not believe."

A week later his disciples were again in the house, and Thomas was with them. Although the doors were shut, Jesus came and stood among them and said, "Peace be with you."

Then he said to Thomas, "Put your finger here and see my hands. Reach out your hand and put it in my side. Do not doubt but believe."

Thomas answered him, "My Lord and my God!"

Jesus said to him, "Have you believed because you have seen me? Blessed are those who have not seen and yet have come to believe."

St. Thomas Aquinas (ca. 1225-1274) has been called the Angelic Doctor for his combination of mighty intellect and deep spirituality. A Dominican, he was the author of *Summa Theologica;* he is also known for his hymns and poems.

Prayer Before Holy Communion

Almighty and ever living God,
    I approach the sacrament of your only-begotten Son,
    our Lord Jesus Christ.
I come sick to the doctor of life,
    unclean to the fountain of mercy,
    blind to the radiance of eternal light,
    and poor and needy to the Lord of heaven and earth.
Lord, in your great generosity,
    heal my sickness, wash away my defilement,
    enlighten my blindness, enrich my poverty,
    and clothe my nakedness.
May I receive the bread of angels,
    the King of kings and Lord of lords,
    with humble reverence;
    with the purity and faith, the repentance and love,
    and the determined purpose
    that will help to bring me to salvation.
I now receive your beloved Son under the veil of a sacrament.
May I one day see him face to face in glory.

St. Thomas More (1478-1535) was a politician and a humanist scholar. As Lord Chancellor of England under Henry VIII, More refused to accept the king as head of the church and was therefore beheaded. In his famous book, *Utopia*, he shows his lack of interest in asceticism.

No Pleasure Forbidden

∞

Dinners in Utopia are very short, but their suppers are somewhat longer, because after dinner comes work, but after supper come sleep and natural rest, which they think are more suited to wholesome and healthful digestion. No supper is passed without music, and their banquets do not lack fancy foods and sweets. They burn incense and perfume spices to scent the air, and they sprinkle about sweet ointments and waters. Indeed, they leave nothing undone that could bring cheer to the company. For they are much inclined to think that no kind of pleasure is forbidden from which no harm comes.

St. Venantius Fortunatus (ca. 535-ca. 605),
Bishop of Poitiers in present-day France, was a poet
and a biographer.

A Hymn to the Cross

∞

*S*ing, my tongue, the song of triumph,
　　Tell the story far and wide;
　　Tell of dread and final battle,
　　Sing of Savior crucified;
　　How upon the cross a victim
　　Vanquishing in death he died.
Faithful Cross, above all other,
　　One and only noble tree,
　　None in foliage, none in blossom,
　　None in fruit your peer may be;
　　Sweet the wood and sweet the iron
　　And your load, most sweet is he.
Bend your boughs, O Tree of glory!
All your rigid branches, bend!
For a while the ancient temper
　　That your birth bestowed, suspend;
　　And the king of earth and heaven
　　Gently on your bosom tend.

St. Vincent Pallotti (1795-1850) was a Roman priest who dedicated his life to works of social justice. He was the pioneer of Catholic Action and founder of the Pallottine Fathers.

God in All

∞

Not the intellect, but God;
   not the will, but God;
   not the soul, but God;
   not taste, but God;
   not touch, but God;
   not the heart, but God;
   not food and drink, but God;
   not clothing, but God;
   not rest in bed, but God;
   not wealth, but God;
   not honor, but God—
God in all and always.

St. Zechariah, was the father of St. John the Baptist. His song, the Benedictus, is a prayer of thanksgiving for John's birth and the promised Messiah. It is found in Luke 1:68-79.

He Has Raised Up a Mighty Savior
∾

Blessed be the Lord God of Israel,
    for he has looked favorably on his people and redeemed them.
He has raised up a mighty savior for us.
Thus he has shown the mercy promised to our ancestors,
    and has remembered his holy covenant,
        the oath that he swore to our ancestor Abraham,
    to grant us that we,
    being rescued from the hands of our enemies,
    might serve him without fear, in holiness and righteousness
    before him all our days.
And you, child, will be called the prophet of the Most High;
    for you will go before the Lord to prepare his ways,
    to give knowledge of salvation to his people
    by the forgiveness of their sins.
By the tender mercy of our God,
    the dawn from on high will break upon us,
    to give light to those who sit in darkness
    and in the shadow of death,
    to guide our feet into the way of peace.

APPENDIX ONE

Acknowledgments

St. Francis de Sales reprinted from *Introduction to the Devout Life,* translated by John K. Ryan, published by Harper & Brothers in 1950.

St. John of the Cross reprinted from *You Set My Spirit Free: A 40-Day Journey in the Company of John of the Cross,* edited by David Hazard, published by Bethany House Publishers in 1994.

St. Brigid, St. Columba, St. Columbanus, and St. Patrick reprinted from *Celtic Christian Spirituality: An Anthology of Medieval and Modern Sources,* translated by Oliver Davies (1995). Used by permission of The Continuum Publishing Company.

St. Catherine of Siena reprinted from *The Communion of Saints: Prayers of the Famous,* edited by Horton Davies. Used by permission of Eerdmans.

St. Isaiah the Solitary, St. John of Karpathos, St. Mark the Ascetic, and St. Neilos the Ascetic reprinted from *The Philokalia,* vol. 1. Used by permission of Faber and Faber, Inc. and Faber and Faber, Ltd.

APPENDIX TWO

SOURCES AND RESOURCES

The excerpts in this book were taken from a wide variety of sources. In some cases I translated them myself; in others, I condensed, adapted, or paraphrased existing translations to make the short excerpts easily understood. Those kept nearly as I found them are listed on the acknowledgments page. If you would like to read more about or by the saints, here are some suggestions to get you started—a mere handful of the books currently available.

LIVES OF THE SAINTS

The granddaddy of all is *Butler's Lives of the Saints*, first published in the eighteenth century. A twelve-volume revised edition is being published by The Liturgical Press, Collegeville, Minnesota; several volumes are now available. *A New Dictionary of Saints* is a catalog of saints based on Butler and also published by The Liturgical Press. It was most recently revised in 1993.

Servant Publications offers *Treasury of Women Saints* (1991) and *The Kiss from the Cross: Saints for Every Kind of Suffering* (1994), as well as two collections of saint's stories written many

153

centuries ago: *The Little Flowers of St. Clare* (1993) and *The Little Flowers of St. Francis* (1985).

Or look for a biography of a saint who interests you. An interesting place to start is G.K. Chesterton's *Saint Francis of Assisi* (New York: Doubleday Image, 1990).

THE EARLIEST CHRISTIANS

For translations of writings from the first three centuries of Christianity, you might want to check out these ancient sources: *The Acts of the Christian Martyrs* (Oxford: Clarendon, 1972); *Documents in Early Christian Thought* (Cambridge, England: Cambridge University Press, 1975); *Early Christian Writings: The Apostolic Fathers* (New York: Penguin Classics, 1968); or— for an eyewitness account—Eusebius' fourth-century *History of the Church* (various editions). Henry Bettenson's well-known *Documents of the Christian Church* (Oxford: OUP, 1962), though it continues to the twentieth century, also offers many important works from the pre-Constantinian era.

SAINTS OF EASTERN CHRISTIANITY

Some of the quotations in this book are from people called saints by the Orthodox churches but not by the Roman Catholic church. For a guide to Orthodox saints, particularly ones of

Greek origin, try the four-volume *Orthodox Saints* by George Poulos (Brookline, Mass.: Holy Cross Press, 1990).

The Philokalia, a collection of texts written between the fourth and fifteenth centuries by saints and spiritual masters of Orthodox Christianity, is a multi-volume work in progress, translated from the Greek and edited by G.E.H. Palmer, Philip Sherrard, and Kallistos Ware (Boston: Faber and Faber). An excellent introduction to Orthodoxy, including many of its saints, is *The Orthodox Way* by Kallistos Ware (Crestwood, N.Y.: St. Vladimir's Seminary Press, 1995). *The Desert Christian: Sayings of the Desert Fathers*, translated by Benedicta Ward (New York: Macmillan, 1975) includes many saints and writings better known in the East than in the West.

PRAYING WITH THE SAINTS

Most of the saints were known as men and women of prayer, so you can expect to find many saints' prayers in general collections such as *The Catholic Prayer Book* (Ann Arbor, Mich.: Servant, 1986), *The New Book of Christian Prayers* (New York: Crossroad, 1986) and *The Oxford Book of Prayer* (Oxford: OUP, 1985).

Servant publishes three prayer collections that are more specific: *Prayers and Meditations of St. Thérèse of Lisieux* (1992), *The Prayers of Saint Francis* (1987), and *Prayers of the Women Mystics* (1992). *Quotable Saints*, also published by Servant (1992), is a potpourri of quotations thematically arranged by Ronda de Sola

Chervin. Saint Mary's Press publishes the *Companions for the Journey* series: small devotional books (*Praying with* ...) including a saint's short biography and fifteen meditations by or about the saint.

For saints'(and others') prayers that can be used in various liturgical seasons and circumstances, check out Liturgy Training Publications' *Sourcebook* series (Chicago). Titles include *Advent, Christmas, Lent, Triduum, Easter, Liturgy, Baptism, Marriage,* and *Death.*

SAINTS OF BRITAIN AND IRELAND

Celtic and other saints from Britain and Ireland are enjoying a wave of popularity. I was charmed by *Celtic Christian Spirituality: An Anthology of Medieval and Modern Sources,* edited by Oliver Davies and Fiona Bowie (New York: Continuum, 1995) and by *Celtic Fire: The Passionate Religious Vision of Ancient Britain and Ireland,* edited by Robert Van de Weyer (New York: Doubleday, 1990). I also enjoyed *The English Spirit: The Little Gidding Anthology of English Spirituality* (Nashville: Abingdon, 1987). In fact, many books about saints are of British origin, including the great Butler's and one of the first, the Venerable Bede's *Ecclesiastical History of the English People* (various editions; completed in 732 or 733).

Women are represented in most collections and books listed here, but it is still a fact that most saints are men and that most women spiritual leaders did not leave writings for future generations. To research female saints, start with *Matrology: A Bibliography of Writings by Christian Women from the First to the Fifteenth Centuries* (New York: Continuum, 1995). Or enjoy Carol Lee Flinders' *Enduring Grace* (San Francisco: Harper, 1993), portraits of seven women mystics; Bridget Mary Meehan's *Praying with Passionate Women: Mystics, Martyrs, and Mentors* (New York: Crossroad, 1995), stories of thirty women of spirit; or *Woman to Woman: An Anthology of Women's Spiritualities* (Collegeville, Minn.: The Liturgical Press, 1993), in which editor Phyllis Zagano has selected writings from fifteen women spanning ten centuries, and the previously mentioned *Treasury of Women Saints* (Ann Arbor, Mich.: Servant, 1991).

PRIMARY SOURCES FOR GENERAL READERS

For an ecumenical introduction to the writings of a dozen saints and forty other Christian spiritual masters, try *Devotional Classics: Selected Readings for Individuals and Groups,* edited by Richard J. Foster and James Bryan Smith (San Francisco: Harper, 1993). It is especially helpful for groups, for whom a study guide is available.

Evangelicals will appreciate *Rekindling the Inner Fire,* a continuing series of devotional paraphrases from spiritual writers including St. Augustine, St. John of the Cross, St. Francis of Assisi, and St. Teresa of Avila.

Anyone who wishes to make a thorough acquaintance with a particular saint can do no better than to find the volume on that saint in the enormous ongoing series, *Classics of Western Spirituality* (Mahwah, N.J.: Paulist Press), which features helpful biographies and excellent translations of representative writings. The series is largely, but not entirely, Christian. Its most popular volume is on Julian of Norwich.

Doubleday Image and Liguori Triumph also publish attractive paperbound volumes of the writings of many of the best-loved saints.

Primary Sources for Research

For in-depth library study of a person or an era, there are many classic series in English translation. Here are some sets you will find in a university library. If you read Greek and Latin, or even French and German, you will have many more sets to choose from.

Ancient Christian Writers: The Works of the Fathers in Translation. Westminster, Maryland: The Newman Press.

Ante-Nicene Fathers, 10 vols.; *Nicene and Post-Nicene Fathers,* 28 vols. Grand Rapids, Mich.: Eerdmans. A facsimile edition of nineteenth-century classics.

Cistercian Fathers and *Cistercian Studies*. Kalamazoo, Mich.: Cistercian Publications.

Fathers of the Church: A New Translation. Washington, DC: Catholic University of America Press.

Library of Christian Classics. Philadelphia: Westminster. Includes helpful commentary as well as documents. Some volumes are now available in paperbound editions.

Loeb Classical Library. Cambridge, Mass.: Harvard University Press.

Records of Civilization: Sources and Studies. New York: Columbia University Press.

Go Fishing

Having listed all these books, I nevertheless believe that the most interesting way to discover the saints is to browse in a library or bookstore, pick up books that look interesting, and begin to read.

Also Available

❧

BREAKFAST WITH THE POPE
Daily Readings
Pope John Paul II
ISBN 0-89283-946-5

BREAKFAST WITH BILLY GRAHAM
Daily Readings
ISBN 0-89283-983-X

BREAKFAST WITH THE ANGELS
Daily Readings
ISBN 0-89283-991-0

Available at bookstores or from:
Servant Publications
Department 209
P.O. Box 7455
Ann Arbor, Michigan 48107

WRITE FOR OUR FREE CATALOG